Letter

MW01100395

 Harcourt

SCHOOL PUBLISHERS

Photos:
Cover, © Harcourt Telescope; p. 2, © Harcourt Telescope; p. 3, © Harcourt Telescope;
p. 4, © Harcourt Telescope; p. 5, © Harcourt Telescope; p. 6, © Harcourt Telescope;
p. 7, Shutterstock; p. 8, © Harcourt Telescope.

Printed in China

ISBN 10: 0-15-358383-5
ISBN 13: 978-0-15-358383-4

Ordering Options
ISBN 10: 0-15-358355-X (Grade K Below-Level Collection)
ISBN 13: 978-0-15-358355-1 (Grade K Below-Level Collection)
ISBN 10: 0-15-360636-3 (package of 5)
ISBN 13: 978-0-15-360636-6 (package of 5)

4 5 6 7 8 9 10 0940 15 14 13 12 11 10 09

u

u

u

u

u

u

u